The Women Who
Gave Up Their Vowels

poems by

Kate Cumiskey

Finishing Line Press
Georgetown, Kentucky

The Women Who
Gave Up Their Vowels

Publisher: Leah Huete de Maines

Editor: Christen Kincaid

Cover photo: The Canovas Photography

Author Photo: The Canovas Photography, Kelly and Courtney Canova, Deland, FL

Cover Design: Elizabeth Maines McCleavy

Order online: www.finishinglinepress.com
        also available on amazon.com

Author inquiries and mail orders:
Finishing Line Press
P. O. Box 1626
Georgetown, Kentucky 40324
U. S. A.

Table of Contents

For my sister, who came every time I called.
Because: the chapel.

I shine not burn
motto, Clan MacKenzie

Candor

Write a poem about the dried flowers hanging from the curtain rod.
Write your mother, your sister's ex-boyfriend, your hemorrhoids.
Write one honest politician you've shaken hands with; then
write Trump. Write about the eleventh grade American
History teacher who wanted to fuck you.

Write the zoology teacher who raped your best friend. Write
developers from Miami and New York raping the estuary.
Write your history; write that fear at 2 a.m. the night
your son overdosed. Write tile beneath your knees.
Write rats in the kitchen, raccoons in the roof, your dog
over the fence, gone all night.

Write the phone not ringing. Write your first fuck,
your latest one. Write the student you wish would just shut
the fuck up and write one paragraph. Write the one who scares you
& the girl you wish somebody would say *hello* to. Write the gay boy
your heart breaks for. Write punching the wall of your bedroom at
sixteen. Write solutions you dream before they slip into the fetid
air. Write a poem.

After listening to my sister read, online, from her new book of poems

On her first day as a full professor I write about our father.
How, when he held her just home from Halifax Hospital
that first afternoon, he was fluent in this.

Light through jalousies on the river side of the house
reflected on concrete block like shells bouncing morning
through salt water. How if Billy Wofford painted those rays

& Dad holding Carol Ann, I could tell you just where he sat
and at what time of day, relative to river & ocean. So
could she. As she imagines our father's arms beneath her,

quiet, she knows she learned right then to look out: closed lips
pursed just so, half-mast lids, dark eyes wishless, blue as peace.

The moon is round today

—for Carol Ann Davis & Fred Haise

my sister writes. She and I have both been thinking of our father
in elliptical ways we do. Yesterday, an astronaut who might have
known him wrote, asked for a picture. *I am old*, he said, *and forget
things. I may have given him an award.* I've written back before
realizing which Apollo he was on, that my father designed a filter
so he and his two friends could breathe their way home. From this
perch on spinning blue I wonder, why did he send them to the Moon?
Because it was there trite & silly: nothing to do with men I knew.
More likely to give us something to cling to when hard times came.

You are here. Look up.

Hard Times was a cow his uncle could not kill after her milk dried up.
She got them through the Depression. Grateful, the orphan, his uncle;
they agreed Hard Times deserved better. This poem is about honor.
The moon is round today, my sister writes.

Favoring boys

Sometimes, in spite of yourself, you miss her vowels. That way of phrasing things that softened the punch. How she always called your grandmother *Mother*, capital M, italicized even in the salt air of the kitchen. If you cared to you might figure out just why she favored your brothers so openly: perhaps it had something to do with Mama Kate. Probably not. Her advice to young parents, *raise boys*, something you & your sister tried to ignore—teaching each other the ways of women.

She was proud of your degrees, ashamed of your work ethic. *Mother expected a house like that*, she'd say, waving her thin, nail-bitten right hand at Riverside Drive estates. Over three bridges to the periwinkle she raised seven children in. How you loved that house. Not talking about it when your brother took a ten-pound sledge to the interior walls two days after her funeral, it felt like you were choking on vowels.

Carol Ann refuses to call them "the boys," as Mother always did—*for God's sake, they're grown men, half of them retired*—but you can't help thinking of them that way: five blond heads, wide blue eyes tearing up at the least little thing. How tough the two of you became, the women who gave up their vowels. Both raising men. Mother blamed you for everything from bad traffic to Donald Trump. You forgive her, as you did, always, before the words were even out of her mouth.

Dirge

You can buy fairy lights for the bedroom, draw the curtains but eventually
sunlight will fade them. The neighbor still pours motor oil on your cactus
garden & cuts down your trees after hurricanes.

You can buy local food, even grow wheat grass and squeeze your own
grapefruit but the Wal-Mart and Hobby Lobby trailers still crack
the earth and cement buffers under railroad ties, stacked two high

when they wake you. The warning blast from the engineer lower at 2 a.m.
than when you wait, patient, behind the barricade by the convenience
store, afternoons.

Blow up your T.V., move to the mountains, dig a basement, buy a
generator. Pretend we don't need you. Pretend none of it matters;
all politicians are crooked; voting rigged. Be lazy—

this is America, it's allowed. Write poems about lichen, waterfalls,
deer graceful as ballerinas through fog at dawn. It's too late. Now
we know America unmasked is Jefferson raping Sally

Hemings, Columbus's cabin boys crying out in the rat-shit dark,
smallpox blankets. Idiots in red hats, screaming *lock her up.*

May 25, 2017

Today is the day my body decides
I miss you. My sinews, bones tire—
and I remember it was strangers you
most loved. Not your children. Today

is the day I come across a picture of Sarah,
head tilted just so in the surfboard room,
and wish for generosity retrograde to infancy.
However. What you gave is beyond my grasp,

and really beyond compare. Your harsh laugh.
Your laser blue glare. If I could just pick up
the phone and hear: *Oh, yeah. Oh yeah.*
I forgive you. Everything. How I wish your

days had been easier. But I wasn't there for
the beginning. Just the middle and the end:
John's eyes, over your sheets & rasp:
his gentle gaze.

Instructions: an elegy

Remember the feel of wood near jalousie panes, separating
bins in the penny candy aisle. Remember dust on terrazzo
at the Beach Variety Store. When you think of Mother,
remember her naps, and cracks in the pavement between
Robinson and Flagler. Summer. The quarter in your pocket.

Sweat on your upper lip and breeze off the Atlantic layering
salt on your skin. Which ended up cool. Spanish bayonets
crowding sidewalks that disappear every block or so. Stickers
in sand between them and the curb. Remember your brother,

lagging behind to observe a creature—possibly water, possibly
land—making its way. As both of you were. As you are, now.

Florida love poem

What I want is to write
about the ocean, how the sand
meets it not far from the end
of Robinson Road, how white
sand coats your feet, damp
under streetlamp and whip
of sea oats in midnight.

Instead, I will make a body poem
with sliding next to my sleeping
husband, wake him almost up,
offer myself as I had not yet learned
to, all those years ago in his cottage
near Flagler Avenue—windows kept
open by lead weights on cotton rope,
pulleys. Salt rusting window screens,
mattress ticking on the living room

floor. How much more he loves
my body now: thickened, heavy,
scarred. Deliberate thing, to wake
a sleeping man, make love after
midnight with work in the morning.
It is the poem I write: the ocean
glowing and rolling under the moon.

For the one that got away

—for Shenandoah

What you want is a wand for family gatherings. Better:
a potion poured in the Scotch, homemade wine, or better
still the gumbo. Vanish stories that fetish, lies the baby
of the family had no voice for or against. Let her

speak, be heard from now: a professor, only academic
in the room. Allow the brother who took French fries
from some stranger's plate his adult manners. The one
who used to hold his breath until he passed out medals

for valor, his calm at sea. Invite those late to the party—
midwestern brother-in-law, felonious nephew—to the table.
Pass the biscuits. Look out the window, see tarpon jumping in
the bay. Let the tarpon be the tarpon jumping in the bay,

not *the one that got away*. Allow your parents their crippling
humanity, their love, and their dying.

Logic knot

She tunes in to Jacob's Twitch on Saturdays when the house is empty
and the dog has snuck into a brown velvet chair in the living room;
does it for the language of the game and just so she can see him
from here to there—third of four, the son who made his first friend

in tenth grade, asked for a fridge for Christmas when he was eleven
so he wouldn't have to see anyone. Ever. The nights of Autism
exhaustion play in a logic knot like the White Album in reverse
while he chats with people from Amsterdam & Coeur de Aleen,

flipping cards like coins in a fountain. She remembers him running
from sculpture to sculpture in the Ringling garden in Sarasota, begging
the docent for something to cover those naked people up after
searching the gallery for Sitting Woman with a Fish Hat. And here

he is, making a living teaching Magic the Gathering to anyone
willing to drop a tip in the virtual box. Hannah—whose name
he points out is a palindrome—makes blueberry pancakes and
contemplates sharing the recipe. This one. This one who crawled

out of his bedroom on his elbows at four, slept with a bag of magnetic
letters, and walked on his toes has a poetry degree, a wife, and a cat
called Morgana. She turns the screen off and lets the sound of his
voice drift past the dog, into the kitchen while she does the dishes.

Poem for Anne Bracewell

The old dog has buried his shit once again at the foot of the bed. This
time, in a shirt bought for your mother when she was in the hospital,

one she'd never wear. Just like her—a man's blue flannel plaid, hung
in the cardboard closet; only thing you took after a nurse let you close

her eyes, clip the plastic bracelet. Goodwill buy, last thing that lit those
blue blue eyes. Old dogs get embarrassed, old ladies die. You read Jo

Ann Beard over and over, understanding as you do plasmasphere,
plasmapause: Self-pity the one thing you will not do.

Jim's Megan

trips into my house,
lovely, unencumbered
by life after four.

Clings to her mother
whose charm Megan wears
as a coat to be grown into.

(Her father's darkling beauty a potion
across her eyes and hair)

She peeks *goodbye* over
a shoulder. The empty
place Megan left wanders
the house, settles by the door.

Place whither

Snake doctors swarm depending on tides; low, sometimes neap.
Never high. At dawn, mourning doves *coo* from telephone wires.
Gopher tortoises crunch stickers on Davis Hill at the end
of Robinson Road. Miss Molly's house long gone, a lone gas line,
capped, sticks out of a sand dune. Sea oats root where they want.
Aloe grows against porches flush with yards.

When hurricanes brush past on their way to North Carolina &
New Jersey, snakes and crabs hole up. It's restful to imagine
this place long after you are gone, or even just away for a bit—
and to picture the sandbar it was, centuries ago, beached starfish
seeping purple up what is now the middle of the street, absent you.

Distance

At forty-two, she finally grasps or at least grasps at the remove past lovers (even friends, especially family) keep others.

Like the boyfriend who always tried to hold his breath instead of crying out. The brother who only calls when he needs

inside advice on a good hotel or when the fish are running. Hides her relief at the daughter up & moving to Halifax,

promising to come back for Christmas. Shoves the dream down of books, bed, table, candle: windy mountaintop anywhere but here.

Just lately I feel my body settling

Just lately, I feel my body settling itself into the shape of Mother's
like a hand in a glove. Not gently, struggling to get there—tight,
sometimes twisted and grasping like white gloves she used to push
my hands into for church; pearlized button and loop on the back
just where the wrist bent to shelter its most delicate aspect. Ribs
of rucked cotton star bursting, or cutout daisies with tissue-thin
skin showing through.

Bit by bit my body settles into age: fractious, screaming all the way
down. Only in twilight sleep I feel my lower jaw shift, relax, offset
to the right, the side I sleep on. My mouth clamps, thin-lipped, crooked,
and settles for sleep into Mother's fighting look, the one she wears
when she will not be moved. Then I can rest. And it feels good,
like falling into my own skin.

Mother is eighty-four. She lives alone, across two bridges and a
causeway in the house my father bought to be close to his rockets,
close to the sea. She leaves the front door unlocked. Back, too. Someday
I will open that door, cross the terrazzo, find her lying on the quilt I made,
T.V. tuned to Rachel Maddow, wearing a new aspect. One I'll settle into
as well, gently or un, one not-too-distant day.

A Florida surfer dumpster-dives in Washington

—for Carol Ann Davis

I've been to Bellingham twice; once through on the train to Vancouver, once to stay three days with Mikel. Enough to be satisfied he has a life there. Now, my imagination is colorized by the Pacific & insular homes huddled gull-like above train tracks north of town. I picture him scrounging books behind some low-slung shop hugging High Street.

He's been to the co-op, wants something to read while he waits for Kelsi at Great Harvest. She kneads. I need to see him here, where surfing is grabbing baggies after school, running down the street. The Gulf stream beckons. Still, there's something in his voice—*I found Aunt Carol Ann, four copies!*—which makes Bellingham okay.

It's easier to imagine Mikel feeding his soul from dumpsters than his body. I don't know why. Bellingham is a baroque poem; green, verdant. There's no denying the pull of water. Here, everything's underwater, flat-brown, hot. Florida is a renga ebbing in mangroves. My boy, my man-boy finds poetry three thousand, two hundred, seventy-one miles away in dumpsters, in lichens and glacial stones worn smooth, cold as beach glass.

In the crepuscular light of the gloaming

I walk with my husband. Not every night but some—we are trying.
We walk late not because of the light, but heat; Florida in August
is mean. Our street, despite bats whipping through pine tops
and glimmer of lightning bugs illuminating live oaks, isn't safe.
No sidewalks, 4.3 miles end-to-end, working folk whip home

in the near-dark. Nefarious activity in the periwinkle houses is common
as dryer-lint scenting air. One house south of home is a foreclosure where
a boy who played with ours is markedly absent. A Homeland Security
sticker on the door; he's serving fifteen years in federal pen for marketing
baby porn. North, the local whorehouse. Good neighbors. they keep the lawn

 perfect, drapes drawn. You hedge your bets, here. This attempt to walk
for health typifies a marriage started at 17. We are still trying. Sometimes,
I reach for his big hand and squeeze the arthritis in rhythm with our steps
from his guitar fingers. Others I pound pavement without him, twenty steps
walking, twenty at a run hoping he wonders if I am okay while I anger myself

out of breath. It is a marriage. It is thirty-two years and counting. Last week
in this same light I heard the blast when a fifteen-year-old with a crush on our
son died. I marked the time as my soldier-husband taught me years ago to do,
not knowing then the perils of this shattering love. Once I asked a neighbor boy,
why do you all gather here? (holes in the roof, dog shit, canned food dinners)

Don't you know, he replied, *yours is the only normal house in the neighborhood?*
Years later, I finally understand. A mom, a dad. There's two parents, here. Last
night, our oldest son called from Bellingham, suspicious when I told him *Dad
and I are trying to lose weight together, walking. It's August,* he said, and though
he did not say so, understood other dangers lurking when I replied, *We walk
in the gloaming.*

Weekends, the teacher drives Uber eats

He sees the lives of buildings as you your own
in dreams. Tenses mix, cease to matter:
Grandmother's hair superimposed on daughters
you didn't have: see her running to catch up with them,
Rachel & Katie Anne. Who forgive you.
        Structures don't
get that chance, but he gives it to them in passing—
redemption mixed with absolution.

Sacramentally speaking, periwinkles lost to McMansions
bring him to tears, speechless. Down U.S. 1 between
the No Name and Tailgators he drives milkshakes,
pancakes to stoners in Redfish Cove.
        It's Saturday morning, and Friends
Bank has been empty two years, three months, six days:
It wants to be a church. Just add a steeple and some Jesus.
Who cast money changers from the temple.

The sick poet

—*after Jane Kenyon*

How good the cold Big Mac tastes from the bottom of the beautiful
brown paper bag. A squabbling couple in the play place doesn't know
how lucky they are. *Let him have all the fries he wants*, she wishes
she could holler. An*d a Coke!* If only

she'd written the way families who look carved out of cream cheese,
plastered on Christmas cards, drove her nuts. She should have burned
them in effigy, not thrown them in a drawer to collect dust. What if—

instead of putting up with—just once she had walked out, boarded a bus
like a character dreamed up by Anne Tyler: clock winder, restaurateur;
somebody brave? Anybody brave. What if she'd written the body,
its foibles and wants?

Church piano bar

—remembering Brother Canova, Edgewater Baptist Church

How if I needed one reason to continue (as sometimes we do) the curve
in the wall behind the choir loft would save me. Just where Sayer Canova
placed his easel, sermon in art illuminating the black velvet in chalk, his
back to us—saving the lightest pastels for last. Jesus wandered hills,
lowcountry, barren places. Revealing, after all, who would save us. John
and me forgetting all about Marlon Perkins' Wild Kingdom, Wonderful

World of Disney. Everybody quiet all the slow way home. Is the curve
in that wall, carefully troweled plaster, where saving began? Once,
the preacher called on John to pray, *Brother John Davis will lead us.*
Quick as that, J. D. replied, *next time I'm home.* Four years and Sayer
didn't miss a beat, *young brother Davis will lead the offertory prayer.*
What do I bring here, third pew from the front on the right, seven feet

from where I stood shaking in my ballet slippers, nineteen, just married?
We knew less than nothing, and church piano bar was as far as whiskey
from a prayer. If I continue, if some Tuesday afternoon find myself
in that pew where I learned to read & sing: rise and run my fingertips
along the plastered curve of wall next to the baptismal, will it save me?
Grace upon grace, just for me?

Her house

smelled like Tide and Prell and Dial soap. Cleaning up she was fast—
things on the floor went in the sink, the washing machine, or the trash.
Rinse your feet with the hose before you come in and you'd better be
careful on the terrazzo. Don't knock, the door's not locked.

Pitcher of tea on the table. Sweet. *Make some ice, Mary Kate.* Reading
could get you out of anything but dinner. Shove a book in the back
pocket of your shorts and you were home free all day. Air-conditioning
was at the bank. In summer, the library across the river smelled like
mold and wet newsprint. It rained every day at three;

if you had sand on your feet you'd better rinse them or get the broom
out of the Florida room and sweep. Sometimes you'd sleep there,
an old blue twin bed with a ticking mattress atop an open box spring.
For the breeze. Sometimes you'd sweat through dreams, about leaving:

about places not like this—close, closed doors, cool. And the beach
whispered with the sea, brushing each other, over, back:
shhhhh. freeeeee. shhhh. freeee.

For breath

This is a poem to breath. Not the lycra-clad
chakra-seeking heated bait,

but breath one waits for
while the world spins, oblivious.

The noxious-sweet breath of one loved in
brighter days: swimming pool, wedding shower.

The aunt who showed you just how to walk like
a lady, and chatted with Mother while you

blew your first bubble, barefoot on the terrazzo
of her foyer. The hospital breathes *hush*. Hospice

one floor up from where she answered archly,
"Please do" when the nurse promised to watch

her grammar. It's downhill from there. Still, breath
is what you want, any breath: rattle, cough, sigh.

And then, ceasing, peace; and you hope, coaxing on,
she's heard you once in the bright brittle days,

forward, as if, as if, you could do it for
her: in, out. Onward.

Poem to the remains found in the woods near Pullman Ave.

—for Ashlyn Bowman, 17

Across the street, your grandmother lies not waiting
anymore. Not quite across—across, and one house north.
On a bit of a rise. With graywater for the lawn, and a garage.
A pool out back. You'll never come home again.
Ashlyn, how I wish I'd stopped and said *hello* the last
time I saw you out front on your skateboard. In a hurry,
I watched you in the rearview mirror. Waiting for something.
What? Eighty-four days before they found you, not far
from a body of water: uncovered, mostly bones.
What I can't stop thinking of is how alone you must
have been in the Florida wet, in the dark, wondering
what you'd done to end up there—wishing
for just one more moment, to tell her something,
anything, to make this easier. How you must
have hurt. How you must have been afraid. And I
your neighbor had no time for you, that last bright
know-nothing do-nothing Florida Shores afternoon:
not fair, not stormy. I wish—

Her mother's books

Tonight, Kelly gives me her mother's books. It's more
than it appears to be. Sea Island waltzing through the Marshes
of Glynn. Then, Mikel will fix her computer. Ghost of Cab-Sab
tickling pages and somebody will go out for a cigarette. Ghosts
of avocado trees Sarah and Delaney hacked to pieces after
Paula died tickle the underside of my chair on the screened-in
porch. I miss you.

Why is meat sweetest, close to the bone? Nights sashaying
over for a glass of wine, a poem. Sometimes, sitting in your
dining room, remembering others—low ceiling, salt air,
Dune Circle and *Cecilia* on the turntable—I realize there's no
one to remember that but me, Mikel, and Kelly, and maybe
we'll laugh with an air of levity we really don't feel,
just to soldier on. Without you.

After Joan Didion

Grief takes time—something our grandmothers knew,
rely on still rooms, warm foods, a limited view. Close
windows. Cover mirrors with something dark
& soft. Hushed talk, or silence.

Don't read or try to. Beware of names and of spicy foods;
keep a reliable neighbor in the kitchen, someone you
need not introduce. Let that person—only that one
manage things, shoo busybodies, answer the door. Keep

toys from the floor; relegate children to a back room.
Grief takes time. Let yourself tire, sleep, steep in warm
baths. Handkerchiefs not tissue when you weep.
Tea with honey, tomato soup & grilled cheese.

Eat. Lie about, shut the door, say *no*, say nothing.
Our grandmothers knew grief takes time, sometimes
forever. You are not you any longer; you've crossed
a room.

What we settled for

—in memory of David Berman

Today on an impromptu ride home from work (air out in the portable during preplanning) your youngest son shared his playlist and drove the green F-150 stick-shift longbed, shy as geckos at midnight under the porch light. Mexican blanket on the bench seat, *Deportees* on the iPod and you wondered about singing. *Goodbye to my Juan, goodbye Rosalita*

more heartbreaking now than when you were 23. If you sing along, will it bother him like it did when he was ten? But you've learned how to listen. In the air a scent like Tallahassee, 1978, how sinkholes just off the byway pushed the smell of hay between long-leaf pines. Cool air, cool as snowmelt. David Berman has

killed himself. As poets will do. Your oldest son knows this—they all do, really, of course, of course—and you sheltered them as you could. Punishment by poetry was supposed to be a joke, a tool meant to soothe on surf trips to North Carolina, Cali. But poetry, music wormed their way in and there's no saving

them now. No matter the sawmill in the carport, vacation Bible school, tossing a ball back and forth with Grandpa Sunday afternoons. Your children sing. I was going to say *sing and dance* but that's just it: there is no dancing, now. El Paso, Orlando, Sandy Hook. A bloody ghost-trail echoing through childhood. Tell yourself they're the lucky ones, your sons. But you will do as other poets have done, blame yourself. As you should. Mother, snarky: *You get what you settle for.* You thought she was talking about boys.

Potting Mother's aloe

When you remove the plants from the coquina flowerbox
take care with roothairs. Lay the aloes on their sides; clean
a pot from nearby in tepid water at the kitchen sink. Carry
them in an old iron pot salvaged from the beachside
when the house was being destroyed from the inside
out; sledgehammers, hired hands.

Let the aloes rest, let them float. Fill clean clay with dirt
from the same holes, filter it with fingertips. Cast away sticks,
bits of concrete block eroded from your mainland house. Place
the longest root in a circle; circumnavigate the interior, muddy
now with life-strings; feed them with dirt and tap water. Lace
bristly stars of aloe against the lip of white enamel bleeding
terra cotta at the rims—ivy faired into the outside. Ivy
that disappears once the plant grows over the edge.

Let that go, too, just like Mother's house. The smallest plant,
grown in the shadow of the other, place exactly center: nucleus.
Anathema for your sentimental wallow, use new snippers
to snap plumeria, blooming, and throw that in the backseat
with the aloe. Drive Old Mission to Pioneer Trail to Glencoe,
place both next to your brother's roses, the thorny ones,
and the dead gardenia. Knock.

Rag & bone

In sleep-late Sunday-morning dreams I stroll the rag and bone shop
of my heart, laced in the shadows with stones, moss-dripped
lichen-riddled things with poetry scratched in. How do they do that?

Yeats was not the Yeats we know when he wrote that; chasm
of loneliness opening, too much time left. In rag and bone times
focus on stones, not the bones beneath. Read poems, make them up
for the girls who died in fire, the sailors and the nuns.

And later make fun of yourself, but in the heart remember how hard
your mother tried to teach you, Sunday afternoons strolling
the burial ground, ready you for death. Enter the shop of my heart,
the nest of my house. Open the door that still says

this is the door you're looking for, little plaque Mikel won't
let me take down or paint over. We have coffee, good coffee,
homemade cakes, bread and butter, oranges in the back yard.
The autism nest in the rag and bone shop of my heart

is filled with music: Psaltery, mouth organ, Laravie and Takamine.
We don't fold laundry. Vertical book stacking is the order of the day
and none of our secrets are on display, but ghosts are there.
My indiscretion, his thumps and shouts. Choose a song, a poem.

Didn't you

feel sorry for the old woman next door who kept finding reasons
to come over, volunteering more than you wanted to know about
your temporary neighborhood? How you love Vacation Rental by
Owner, it makes you feel at home and a smart shopper. This time,
you tried to unload the pod full of your parents' things without
a tear. Not a vacation. A weekend to meet and divide fifty years,
three homes, seven children's things. Rocket drawings, love letters.

Apollo skin trapped in Lucite, our oldest brother's hair in an envelope.
Chairs. Box after box of books, photographs shoved into albums every
which-a-way. Stainless steel potato masher, blond wooden toilet paper
spindle. Poetry. Cast iron frying pan. She just stood there, yammering,
certain you were up to no good. Or, moving in. *No loud music. No pot
parties. You can't imagine what we put up with—this is a good
neighborhood.* Mosquitoes buzzing through the garage, pic burning

on a green saucer. Of course, you thought of Mother, alone over on
the beachside those years after we were gone, pile of mysteries
on the bedside table you put together one trip home. Which you set
carefully down in that strange garage, not hers, not your own. Not
the property of the Ohio-transplant standing hipshot three feet away,
doing her best in the Florida heat, sure of nothing. Like you. Like me.
Family photos, not ours, just inside the kitchen door. Philip, we're all

traveling to the same place; and these things barely cover hearts raw with
fear, pumping, soldiering on.

Young for scars

John Lennon glasses, spiky hair, Danny Kaye moves
tap tapping Vera Allen on a 1950s club dock jutting
into trumpet song. Tulle, Italian wingtips, martini.
A parlor trick: drop his name in the groove downtown
late night, they bring you comfort food, company.

Shortcut. Just a way of putting your server, barback
in Jimmy's club. How he threw himself in front of every
ball, hoping for the best. Measured the rim to the bowl
with glittery eyes and dropped: front of the pack, blissfully
paddling through bait balls, too. Leaders sleep alone,
but more, he's the sort snatching tongs from a fire, giving
away waves & heart & higher things: pennies from his pocket,
smiles like Florida sun. See the scars where the surgeon

tried to hide them when he gets tickled, can't help himself,
laughing like there's no tomorrow, just over his lip
where face meets air. And his arms, ropy Mick Jagger
grace-dripping things, covered:
oil burn, knife-cut, honey-honed sugar sticky
worn right through, scarred over. He's out there.

But when the ER doc slips the needle in for a digital block—
just a few stitches this time, shark-nip, close call—
you see tears shimmering, red-eye, free fall.

The cell phone dictionaries

Between two English classes on the backside of Daytona High is an office meant to hide students during shootings. Bookshelf, two desks, bootleg mini-fridge. Doors lock from the inside. Early mornings from the breezeway you can watch the sun rise

and hawks eyeing squirrels and rats from the hurricane fence around the ball fields. I'm here because of a threat at another school—safer to transfer than let the kid know I know the note was about me—and both women I teach with despise me. Venom like spit foaming after a coral snake bite. All orange and black and white. Everything bleached out or technicolor; because I publish. Because teaching hasn't killed me yet.

I go in early for the hawks, the smells, alone time with books. And find, scattered across red chart paper on the office floor, our set of Merriam Websters: old, that red cloth-cover, tenth edition. Five of them. A jiffy-cutter, unhoused, a plastic tray of glue congealed, brushes trapped like ducks in quicksand. The bitch who teaches next door comes in, sees my face, brightens, *I'm using them for cell phone jail! See?* then, not so sure, lies through her big white teeth: *I got them at Goodwill.*

The children have glued pages, knifed out the centers, but I take them home anyway: after school dictionary rescue, imagining burial, burning, drinking words like wine from the holes' margins.

Over Christmas break, my student's boat burns

~Somewhere a white horse gallops with its mane
plunging round a field whose sticks
are ringed with barbed wire

                         Derek Wolcott

Sixth is my rowdiest class. Thirty-two students in a portable in back
of the baseball field. After lunch, half of them stoned, half
late so go to the door, unlock it, let them in. Over &
over. Because of shooters. Someone might come to hurt

me, or the children I try to teach poetry. With each *taptaptap*: Stop.
Plod to the door, bend, peer through the space made by the orange file
folder drop-down shade I've taped up, open, stand aside, plod to the podium,
resume. We've been eating Williams' plums, musing what *depends*
upon the poet. The government is shut down and Ethan, who sits
in back, black hair a Wolcott's pony forelock, leans out

to tell me, "my boat burned to the waterline in the Inlet
over the break." I think, *write THAT* but I'm in this with heart
& we listen openmouthed while he tells how—out at Shark Shallows—
he left his parents and sisters, swam to the New Smyrna side

of Ponce Inlet because the Coast Guard Station is there.
Nobody home. People on wave skis and Boston Whalers
brought his family in. What do I tell these children depends
upon them?

Sleeptalking

Through the wall I hear you mutter to yourself in the dark. At first
I thought, *one of the children called*, then realized it was just you.
As it's been for some time now (just us).

In the living room I listen to the old dog snore and my right lung sigh.
That's scary, that late-night-whisper lung sound. As a child I often woke
to my father's hand inches from my face, checking for breath.

He's dead now and I recall this; the rocket scientist slipping room to room,
checking his children, their mother. His parents died of pneumonia and he
seemed to me irrational about this. He wasn't, really.

I remember being grateful he wasn't there when Mother died of it.
He'd known she would, all those years ago. Sight impolite to discuss,
we did it only silently—the others never knew we talked

it over while they were reading, watching TV. Even so, we felt guilty;
elaborate code—left certain things unsaid; plane crashes, terrorist attacks.
And death, a familiar wandering the next room. Lung sound, sigh.

Make it white noise

Turn it all off. More—bash a sim before you walk
in the door. No mantras needed. Find a chair. Open
your mouth without studied pause, see what flowers
into the room. Books. People. An open window. Chalk.
Paper is a renewable resource. Park your easy
judgements—go for hard. Accept the person next to
you as if you aren't even in the room.

July 20th, 2018, 9:38 a.m.—dead low tide, the New Smyrna side of Ponce Inlet

Newscasters have come from all over Central Florida to report live; early this morning a young manatee beached herself. They set up cameras well away from the water on tripods, behind vans. The beach is crowded. People fish from the end of the jetty, surfers wait for offshore wind to carve barrels. The water's blue at the margin of the jetty in the tidepool; stingrays bury themselves, egrets argue. Seahawks use both beaks to stab fish then perch on wooden poles, waiting for them to die.

It's cloudy. A storm is blowing in from the west. Last night, we showed our three-year-old grandson the jetty. He's just moved from the Pacific northwest. Fritz loves white sand, sloughs, the drive-on beach. We pinch ourselves. He's here; remark how focused he is on digging, pouring, the changing colors of the sea under cloud and sun. We see green eyes widen when he struggles to stay awake. He's *beached-out.*

Last night in twilight while his father considered surfing between jettys, something moved slow, closer to the shore than dolphins feeding where the current rushes. We told Fritz, *manatee. Sea cow.* It was probably her, the one who beached herself at dawn. Everybody wants to know why she stayed when the tide went out. Here, where she lay, the beach curves toward the Indian River. Cars can't come; dogs are allowed if leashed. Swimming is asinine; the current so swift on out-going tides even the Coast Guard cutter waiting on the river wouldn't reach you in time. Every summer, somebody dies. Ovilles or yankees, five of them, wade on the bar.

South of the jetty, cars crowd up to the high-tide poles. Coolers, surfboards, guitars, woofers, towels, diapers. Easy-ups and umbrellas that screw into sand. And newscasters from channels 2, 6, 9, 11, and 35. The manatee survives—dug out and rescued by the Fish and Wildlife Commission. A cheer goes up when her dinner-plate tail flaps and she drops into deep water. The reporters break down their equipment. Somewhere between here and the TV stations, immigrant three-year-olds—brown-eyed Fritzes—wait in cages; wrapped in mylar, swallowing the salty snot of terror. But the real action is here, right? Right?

Step by step

—for Carol Ann Davis, a response to brick by brick

I walk with your hand in mine now only in dreams, never in mind awake
with butterflies flittering next to Mother's house or mourning doves calling
from the too-low power line to her cat. Sandy Hook un-moored you into
your own sea, salt rising to keep your word ship afloat.

When you were small Mikel and I often forgot you in the backseat
of the Fiesta on dates up to Daytona. *But we gave you Chinese noodles!*
I want to say, *we got you out of the house.* But did we, really, contained
as you already were, determined ponytail wrapped in whatever elastic

thing was handy? *Hurry, hurry, let's go*, but out was already inside you.
Only the coastalness of East rests outside now, that and Luke's
eyes—our father transmuted, hopeful, arrested; accepting all
that has been, all yet to come.

Escape velocity

What we all try for, slipping our own skin like
an Atlas Centaur arching above the cracks
in the driveway. That, too, an illusion—
escape velocity a wish, a dream, yesterday's
news. Now, it's all about near Earth
orbit. How easy to understand, child's play,

the way the Moon pulls harder than our
blue planet, eventually. How it draws
us in its closest ellipse, stirring
sediment, quickening blood. You'd

think we'd think about it, but nobody
does. Cigarette machines, phone booths,
Saturn Vs junk hardware. Whatever
made you think, Dad, we'd get to Venus
when you were around for Emmitt
Till, George Wallace? Now

we have a Space Force, but our names
etched in gold are interstellar. At least
there's that.

11th grade IB, a found poem

*With a graphic description
of the agonized suffering
of a soldier who has inhaled
poisonous gas, Wilfred
Owen reveals the resentment
the World War I soldier had
for the pre-war propagandist
who used Horace's poem to
profess that dying for one's
country would be
         "sweet and becoming."*

*Shakespeare playfully asserts
that when spring arrives
with all the lovely signs
of new life and procreation
everywhere to be seen,
the married man's paranoia
about his wife's possible
infidelity is highlighted by
the cuckoo bird's song
sounding to him like* cuckold,
         cuckold, cuckold.

Love is a verb

Bite your lip when your vegan sister-in-law, helping
herself to the casserole you made, tells your sons
in sing-song, *just remember, meat is murder!*

Remember your grandmother, where your manners
came from. She'd say, *pity her.* Tea sweet enough to make
your molars ache, tomato slices at every meal. How

you wish she were here, could help you with the long
view. Scoop macaroni and cheese; serve from the left.
Let the children charm and laugh, the ones half

the neighbors and most of your relatives claim they
brought up. Take it as a compliment.

The deniers

Because it's easier for you, okay.
Tell yourself, people die every day
all kinds of ways. Pretend you'd

feel perfectly okay hedging your bets
with a five-year-old, yellow bus,
art class, P. E. field. Victoria Soto
died wrapped around somebody's
child. Not yours. And the body

sounds of children trying not to move
in closets is nothing like anything
you know.

Winter

You watch a program about glacier lilies and pikas,
I try to write a poem about all the homeless kids
but they weren't homeless, they lived here who
slept on that couch over the years. It fails.

How do you pen hoarded food, stomach issues?
The elegant dance of dinnertime, downplaying
parenthood? You flip the channel, draw
the line at bison fucking. Instead, it's salmon

who beat themselves bloody on river stones,
refraction a paintbrush of remove. How
thoughtless, spawning. There's no sheltering
our issue from the wild, wild world.

I don't know

If I wrote a poem to you of the years of fits
and darkness, could you read it? A poem
which knocked you in the back of the head
from behind when you were only going
to the kitchen for a glass of milk?
A poem like Mikel carrying Sam from
the front yard after he was dumped
in the ditch, dead-legged, and there
was that third hip—as he called it forever—
until one of the boys who gave it to him
exploded his heart with cocaine? And they
held a party in Samsula like he had done
good things? A poem like that: could you
read it? Say it? Listen without tears
running down your face like they never
could, the days you said, *I'm sorry;*
the nights I lay still as I could, our oldest
son's hand quivering in mine, hoping
you'd just fall asleep?

The things we do not say

I remember it was a urologist
told me how to strip the remaining pee
from my penis by using my finger's
pressure just back of the balls
         —Robert Creeley, from the poem "memory"

How we leave them out. But if I said, *shit himself*
in a poem, a reader's breath might catch in relief;
a hundred others cringe in disgust. Philip Roth pissed
me off with The Breast—what a pig—yet don't you
admire that he displays pork on the page?
And the passage of honor where he cleans
his father stops me; a writer a writer a writer.
He tries to say it, almost does: the graceful God
who allows this. You wipe shit from the walls,
thankful to all that's holy you can.
We all shit ourselves. If you haven't, you will.
Creeley milked urine from his tired old dick
and put that on a page. He did that for you, me,
generosity for our midnight struggles. I held
my brother's eleven-year-old penis while tears
of rage bled to the hospital pillow; this boy
who would become the most dignified of men,
unable to wait any longer even though I begged
for help at the nurse's station. The sound of piss
hitting the bottom of the stainless-steel pitcher left
for it turned me poet, twisting me into something
unafraid of love. All its misery, all its humbling grace.

The vanity of the wait

In the wait you believe it's the hardest part—joke
with your friends on social media about pajamas,

diet. Virtual gatherings and virtual trips; toilet
paper. Until a cough through the wall at midnight

brings you running, then to your knees on terrazzo.
How you envy the vanity of the wait. Wish

you lived in a blue state. How you hold breath
like toxin, like poison you could suck from air

just for him.

In the empty town

I.
Birds are bolder. Raccoons cross yards in the middle of the afternoon.
They know already; everything's changed. Most of the storefront signs

are handmade, just like "missing kitten" and "lost dog" used to be. Don't
you wish someone would run into their front yard and start screaming?

Yesterday an accident happened on the freeway: three dead, nobody came.
The whole thing playing out with just a pair of rookie cops in handmade

masks, rescue workers busy elsewhere. News services broadcast free
on the internet, yet *Pennysavers* still pile up at the foot of the driveway.

Who does that? Who still comes, pre-dawn, to throw papers wrapped
in possibly-deadly plastic, all over the empty town? Remember

your grandmother never talked about her childhood polio.

II.
Didn't try to hide it, matter-of-fact, what's the point in bringing
up old news? She wore one elevator shoe. Once, spending a week

in Atlanta you saw her undressed, slip, unhooking her stockings
before a nap. Saw the shoe, the limp to the bathroom. Closed door.

And one Florida noon, asked Mother. She used a National Geographic
to teach you about the polio epidemic. Suddenly, you understood

Mama Kate's iron attitude, courtly manner, stubborn Southern chin.
She lived the limping life of the lucky—as do you.

As do you.

How are you?

I had a friend who answered honestly. If you didn't want to know, you learned not to ask. Jim made it practice to never lie. Tougher than you'd think; possibly cruel. He wanted to live without regrets. Jim died a horrible death, foggy-minded, unable to sweat. When I was large with Sam, our second son, rolling from behind the steering wheel of the blue Buick and climbing the firehouse steps, he laughed, *Mikel didn't tell me you were so tiny.* Meant it. Face like an imperial pirate, voice of a diplomat. We need new greetings. *How are you?* doesn't work anymore, if it ever did. Who wants to hear about night sweats, loneliness? Something Gaelic might do. Words that show you hold no grudge, come in peace. Helloing the house suddenly courtly, elegant. How we learn.

A mushy heart

Today I am sick at heart, tired of phone calls
from thoughtless children of privilege, of
their first-world problems. Tired of the loneliness
of the lonely.

I want to find a home for my friend's novel.
He suffers from a heart too big and had the gall
to have a stroke. Now he can't read and his wife
is distraught; it's all too much. She hasn't
forgotten he got her through three kinds of
cancer—but can't take him anywhere. He eats
French fries off other diners' plates without
asking. Then, he's sorry.

Mother had a friend with a mushy heart
whose second husband loved her to distraction.
They were happy seven years before it killed her.
She was dead before her soft blond curls hit
the floor. I don't know how he is.

Why do people only call when they need you?
The fiction of luxury of choice drives me batshit;
that you're so strong they can pick and choose
like unripe fruit, put you in a brown paper bag
on the kitchen windowsill. Consume at will.

Nowadays, the wolf is at the door and rats roam
kitchens in broad daylight. Hearts are breaking all
over the planet and CNN scrolls the #s on the right
side of the screen, once in a while reminding
viewers, *every one of those is a person*. You'd
have to turn on the volume or closed captioning
to catch that.

Acknowledgements

The author gratefully acknowledges publication of some poems in these fine literary magazines:

Candor in High Shelf VII, July, 2019. High Shelf Press

After listening to my sister read online from her new book of poems and

The Moon is round today, my sister writes in Superstition Review, Issue 23, May 2019

Sleeptalking, During Christmas break, my student's boat burns, and **Dirge** in a forthcoming issue of Green Briar Review

Florida Love poem, Just lately I feel my body settling, Poem for Anne Bracewell (which Raw Art generously awarded an Honorable Mention in the 2019 Doug Draime Prize for Poetry contest), in *The Raw Art Review; A Journal of Storm and Urge*; Spring 2020

For the one that got away, *Crosswinds Poetry Journal*, Volume V 2020

Winter *Forbidden Peak Press, Issue #2: Poetry, Prose, Travel,* and was included in *Spread the Word: A Pandemic Open Mic Anthology*, Jacar Press, February 2021

These are not easy poems, not as we say in the Cumiskey house, "happy little clouds." I'm unsure how to thank those who faithfully and fearlessly read, listen, remind me to eat and sleep when I'm deep in it. My readers, abiding friends and very fine people, all: Shawn McKaig, Summer Perkins, Joan Sberro, Connie Sphire. Courtney and Kelly Canova, whose patience with me is only outdone by their beautiful work. Peter Meinke and Marjory Wentworth, for taking the time to read my poems, consider them, and speak. My sister Carol Ann, whose devotion to craft is a humbling reminder to do the work. Mikel and our four sons and their partners ground me and daily remind me how lovely humans can be. Mikel, a deep curtsey for your unflagging patience. Want to hear a new poem?

Kate Cumiskey is a writer, painter, and social justice activist living with her husband Mikel in coastal Central Florida. There, they raised four sons together, choosing to stay close to their families. Cumiskey's parents moved with the space program from her native Alabama when she was three years old. Her father was a lead designer for NASA for more than twenty years. Cumiskey holds a Bachelor's in Education from the University of Florida and a Master of Fine Arts from the University of North Carolina, Wilmington. While there, she studied with Mark Cox, Philip Gerard, and Clyde Edgerton; as well as her friend the late Robert Creeley, Nick Flynn, and Mark Doty. She met Creeley at Atlantic Center for the Arts in 1994, where she also worked with Peter Meinke and Carolyn Kizer, and where she served as Poet in Residence for a time. Cumiskey pursued post-graduate studies in Creative Writing and Studio Arts at the University of Central Florida. Her work appears regularly in literary magazines and peer-reviewed journals; this is her fourth book. She worked in the public school system as a clerk, teacher, and administrator until leaving in 2020 to pursue her arts full-time. She is the recipient of the State of Florida Best and Brightest Scholarship twice running, an honor earned by less than one percent of Florida teachers. She is recognized by the National Association of Social Workers for her pioneering work in the field of Autism Spectrum Disorders. Cumiskey served the state of Florida as Coordinator of Educational Training Programs at the Center for Autism and Related Disabilities at the University of Central Florida, where she also taught Creative Nonfiction. She designed and presented trainings for parents, teachers, doctors, lifeguards, and families. Cumiskey presents regularly at local, national, and international conferences including: The Association of Writers and Writing Programs conferences, The Florida Historical Society's Annual Meeting, and the Florida Arts in Education Summit. She is active in local community arts programs, including judging poetry contests for Atlantic Center for the Arts and the local public libraries. She serves on the Volusia Cultural Alliance Board, and has founded several public-service organizations, including the Independent Student Cadre and the Club for Autism Awareness and Acceptance in her local school district. She has trained other educators in how to plan for and serve homeless high school students—without forcing them to self-identify—while respecting privacy and reserving judgment on students and their families. She and her husband have been blessed to host many independent teens and young adults at their home, and to learn from them the absolute beauty of the human spirit.

www.ingramcontent.com/pod-product-compliance
Lightning Source LLC
Chambersburg PA
CBHW021205090426
42740CB00008B/1232